INCARNATION, INCLUSION, AND INTENSIFICATION

Witness Lee

Living Stream Ministry
Anaheim, California • www.lsm.org

© 1996 Living Stream Ministry

All rights reserved. No part of this work may be reproduced or transmitted in any form or by any means—graphic, electronic, or mechanical, including photocopying, recording, or information storage and retrieval systems—without written permission from the publisher.

First Edition, September 1996.

ISBN 978-1-57593-324-5

Published by

Living Stream Ministry
2431 La Palma Avenue, Anaheim, CA 92801 U.S.A.
P. O. Box 2121, Anaheim, CA 92814 U.S.A.

Printed in the United States of America
08 09 10 11 12 13 / 10 9 8 7 6 5 4

CONTENTS

Title	Page
Preface	5
1 Incarnation, Inclusion, and Intensification (1)	7
2 Incarnation, Inclusion, and Intensification (2)	13
3 An Extract of the Basic Divine Revelation in the Holy Scriptures	23
4 The God-men's Divine Right to Participate in God's Divinity	39

PREFACE

This book is composed of messages given by Brother Witness Lee in Anaheim, California in April and June 1996.

CHAPTER ONE

INCARNATION, INCLUSION, AND INTENSIFICATION

(1)

Scripture Reading: John 1:14; 1 Cor. 15:45b; Exo. 30:23-25; Rev. 5:6

In this message we will begin to consider the three stages of Christ, that is, the three periods of the history of what Christ is—incarnation, inclusion, and intensification. Many believers in Christ know something about the first stage of Christ's history, the stage of incarnation, but they know very little, if anything, about the second and third stages, the stages of inclusion and intensification.

INCARNATION

Christians have paid a great deal of attention to the matter of incarnation. Every year at Christmas so many believers celebrate the Lord's incarnation; however, not many realize what the intrinsic significance of the incarnation is. Through incarnation Christ as God became flesh. John 1:14 tells us that the Word, who is the very God, became flesh.

INCLUSION

In His resurrection the Christ who had become flesh through incarnation became the life-giving Spirit (1 Cor. 15:45b). Christ, therefore, has had two becomings. The first becoming is seen in John 1:14—the Word became flesh. The second becoming is seen in 1 Corinthians 15:45b—the last Adam (Christ in the flesh) became the life-giving Spirit. From our study of the Bible we have found out that Christ's second becoming in resurrection is no less important than His first becoming in incarnation. As we will see, Christ's becoming the life-giving Spirit in resurrection involves something that we may designate by the word *inclusion*.

Anointed with the Life-giving Spirit

Christ's becoming flesh through incarnation was rather simple, for it involved just two parties—the Holy Spirit and a human virgin (Luke 1:26-27, 30-32, 35). Christ's becoming the life-giving Spirit, on the contrary, was not simple, for it involved and included divinity, humanity, Christ's death with its effectiveness, and Christ's resurrection with its power. In and through Christ's resurrection six things were compounded together to become the life-giving Spirit, which is God's anointing ointment (1 John 2:20, 27).

The Bible tells us that God has anointed us with His Spirit (2 Cor. 1:21; Luke 4:18). However, God has anointed us not merely with the Spirit of God (Gen. 1:2) nor with the Spirit of Jehovah (Judg. 3:10; 6:34) nor the Holy Spirit (Matt. 1:18, 20); rather, God has anointed us with the life-giving Spirit, the Spirit who gives the divine life to fallen humanity. Thank the Lord that we all have been anointed by and with this compound life-giving Spirit!

The Compound Spirit Typified by the Anointing Ointment

The compound life-giving Spirit is typified by the anointing ointment in Exodus 30:23-25. Without these verses in Exodus 30, it would be difficult for us to understand how the life-giving Spirit has been compounded with God, man, Christ's death, Christ's resurrection, the effectiveness of Christ's death, and the power of Christ's resurrection.

I am very thankful to the Lord for opening up the details of Exodus 30:23-25 to us in His recovery. When I was with the Brethren, I was taught only that the holy anointing ointment in Exodus 30 refers to the Spirit. This was the only help I received from them regarding these verses. Through the years I have spent much time on these few verses, considering every point, even every word. Each detail

INCARNATION, INCLUSION, INTENSIFICATION

was like a piece of a jigsaw puzzle. Eventually, I was able to put all the puzzle pieces together, and I saw a marvelous picture of the compound Spirit.

The anointing ointment in Exodus was a compound of one main item—a hin of olive oil—compounded with four kinds of spices: myrrh, cinnamon, calamus, and cassia. To be sure, the one hin of olive oil signifies God. The number one signifies God, and the number four (four spices) signifies man as God's creature. In particular, here the number four signifies the incarnated Christ as a human being. Myrrh signifies Christ's death, and cinnamon signifies the sweet effectiveness of Christ's death. Calamus is a reed that grows in a marsh or muddy place, shooting upward toward the sky; thus calamus signifies Christ's resurrection. Cassia is a kind of bark used as a repellent to repel snakes and insects. Therefore, cassia signifies the power, especially the repelling power, of Christ's resurrection.

With the anointing oil in Exodus 30, we also have the number three (signifying the Triune God), seen in the fact that the quantity of the spices involved three units, each of five hundred shekels: myrrh—five hundred shekels; cinnamon—two hundred fifty shekels; calamus—two hundred fifty shekels; and cassia—five hundred shekels. The second unit of five hundred shekels was split into two parts, each of two hundred fifty shekels. These two parts typify Christ, the middle of the Divine Trinity, who was "split," wounded, on the cross. Here we see not only the Trinity (signified by the three units of five hundred shekels each) but also the Christ who was wounded on the cross (signified by the splitting of the second unit of five hundred shekels into two halves of two hundred fifty shekels each). How marvelous is this type!

Furthermore, with this compound ointment we also see the number five, formed in two ways: by adding one hin of olive oil and four spices and in the five hundred shekels. In the Bible the number five signifies responsibility. For example, the Ten Commandments were written on two tablets, with five commandments on each tablet, and the ten virgins in Matthew 25 are divided into two groups of five. Five is composed of four plus one, with the number four signifying man as God's creature and the number one signifying God. From this we can see that the number five signifies God added to man to give us the ability to bear responsibility. In the compound Spirit we have the ability to bear responsibility.

The Compounding of the Spirit Being a Matter of Inclusion

What we have in Exodus 30 is the compound ointment as a type of the compound life-giving Spirit. The actual compounding of the Spirit took place in Christ's resurrection. It was in resurrection that the very God embodied in Christ and mingled with His humanity was compounded with Christ's death, the effectiveness of Christ's death, Christ's resurrection, and the power of His resurrection to produce the compound Spirit. This compounding was a matter of inclusion, for in the compound life-giving Spirit six items are included. Hence, the life-giving Spirit may be called the all-inclusive Spirit, the Spirit who includes divinity, humanity, the death of Christ and its effectiveness, and the resurrection of Christ and its power.

The Spirit Breathed into the Disciples

Whereas the incarnation was an objective matter, this inclusion is subjective to us and applicable to us in our experience. According to John 20:22 in the evening of the day of His resurrection, the Lord Jesus came as the compound Spirit and breathed into the disciples, saying, "Receive the Holy Spirit." Because the disciples were the representatives of the Body, we all were present when the Spirit was breathed into them. At that time the Spirit was breathed into the whole Body. Just as the arm may receive an injection for the benefit of our physical body, so the disciples in John 20 received the Spirit for the whole Body of Christ. As a part of the Body, those disciples represented the Body in receiving the inclusion, in receiving the compound Spirit. Because we can experience Christ in the stage of inclusion in such a subjective way, in this stage He is more applicable to us than He was in the stage of incarnation.

INTENSIFICATION

Not too long after the church was formed, it became degraded. The church should issue in the Body of Christ, but regrettably, as the Epistles reveal, the church gradually became degraded, even at Paul's time. Because of this degradation, the compound life-giving Spirit was intensified sevenfold to become the sevenfold intensified Spirit (Rev. 1:4; 5:6). This sevenfold intensified Spirit is for the overcoming of the degradation of the church and the producing of the overcomers so that the Body of Christ can be built up in a practical way to consummate the New Jerusalem, which is the unique and eternal goal of God's heart's desire.

From the foregoing we can see the history of Christ in three stages: incarnation, inclusion, and intensification. In the first stage—incarnation—Christ was the Christ in the flesh. In the second stage—inclusion—Christ is the pneumatic Christ, the life-giving Spirit. Now in the third stage—intensification—Christ is the sevenfold intensified Spirit. We need to know Christ in all three stages. If we know the three stages of incarnation, inclusion, and intensification, we will truly know the Bible.

CHAPTER TWO

INCARNATION, INCLUSION, AND INTENSIFICATION

(2)

Scripture Reading: John 1:14; 1 Cor. 15:45b; John 20:22; Rev. 1:4; 5:6

In the previous message we began to consider the three stages of Christ. In this message I have the burden to give a particular and up-to-date message on Christ in the three stages of incarnation, inclusion, and intensification.

A WONDERFUL PERSON IN THREE STAGES

If we would know Christ in these three stages, we need to consider the whole Bible. The Old Testament contains many types and prophecies concerning Christ, the Messiah, the coming One. In the New Testament we have the fulfillment of the types and prophecies regarding Christ in the Old Testament. (We have considered these in detail in *The Conclusion of the New Testament,* Messages 34 through 45.) The whole New Testament is concerned with one person—Christ. The New Testament clearly reveals that as the fulfillment of the types and prophecies in the Old Testament, Christ is a wonderful person in three stages. As the wonderful One He is deep, mysterious, and very complicated.

The First Stage—Incarnation— the Stage of Christ in the Flesh

Throughout the centuries the New Testament has been read, studied, and investigated by millions of people. I myself have been reading and studying the New Testament for seventy years. My study has been in three stages: the first stage in mainland China, the second stage in Taiwan, and the third stage in the United States. When I was in China I was greatly helped, even tutored, by Brother Nee. I studied every book of the New Testament and also many different interpretations of the Scriptures. Although I was helped to the uttermost by Brother Nee, while I was in China, my study was limited mainly to the first stage of Christ, that is, the stage of Christ in the flesh, Christ in His incarnation.

As the record of the four Gospels indicates, this stage lasted only thirty-three and a half years. This was the time in which the Lord Jesus accomplished God's redemption judicially. The four Gospels reveal Christ in the flesh as the One who lived a human life on earth and who was then crucified, dying for our sins in order to redeem us back to God. Strictly speaking, this is a matter not of salvation but of judicial redemption.

God's judicial redemption includes the forgiveness of sins (Luke 24:47), the washing away of sins (Heb. 1:3), justification (Rom. 3:24-25), reconciliation to God (Rom. 5:10a), and positional sanctification (1 Cor. 1:2; Heb. 13:12). In a judicial sense, one who has been forgiven, washed, justified by God, reconciled to God, and sanctified unto God is a saved person.

This judicial redemption is not God's full salvation. Rather, judicial redemption is simply the initial part, the foundational part, of God's full salvation; it is the base upon which God's complete, organic salvation is built.

The Second Stage—Inclusion—
the Stage of Christ as the Life-giving Spirit

At this juncture we need to consider the way the four Gospels end. The Gospels end with a record regarding the resurrected Christ who has become the all-inclusive, compound, life-giving Spirit. In the evening of the day of His resurrection, this One came back to His disciples in an altogether mystical way (John 20:19-22). We cannot say that He appeared to them merely in a spiritual way, because He still had a body of flesh and bones. He said to them, "See My hands and My feet, that it is I Myself. Touch Me and see, for a spirit does not have flesh and bones as you behold Me having." And when He had said this, He showed them His hands and His feet (Luke 24:39-40). The disciples could see the mark of the nails in His hands and touch His body. Although the resurrected Christ had a body of flesh and bones that could be seen and touched, He suddenly appeared to the disciples without coming through a door (John 20:19). He did not knock on the door, and no one opened the door, yet He came and stood in their midst. His coming in this way was actually His appearing, His manifestation (21:1, 14). He appeared suddenly to the disciples and then He disappeared suddenly. Although the Lord Jesus had a physical body, He suddenly appeared in the room where the doors were shut. His appearing and disappearing at the end of the four Gospels is not merely spiritual; it is mystical, something that no one can explain.

The Pneumatic Christ

John 20:22 says, "He breathed into them and said to them, Receive the Holy Spirit." This word indicates that Christ was there with the disciples not only in a physical way but also as the life-giving Spirit (1 Cor. 15:45b), as the pneumatic Christ. If He had been present only physically and not as the Spirit, His disciples could not have received Him as the holy pneuma, the holy breath. If the Lord had not come to them as the Spirit, they could have touched His physical body of flesh and bones and they could have embraced Him, but they could not have received Him by breathing Him in. In John 20 the resurrected Christ exhaled, breathing Himself out, and the disciples inhaled, breathing Him in. This indicates strongly that in resurrection He has become the pneumatic Christ, the Christ who is the life-giving Spirit.

In resurrection Christ as the last Adam in the flesh became the life-giving Spirit. This life-giving Spirit is not simple, for this Spirit includes divinity, humanity, death, and resurrection. The Christ who appeared to the disciples in John 20 had four elements as four factors and four qualifications. He was God with the element of divinity and He was a man with the elements of humanity, death, and resurrection. As the One who had become the life-giving Spirit in resurrection, He had these four factors.

The Compound Spirit

This life-giving Spirit is the all-inclusive, compound Spirit typified by the compound anointing ointment in Exodus 30:23-25. Now the Spirit is no longer just the Spirit of God typified by the olive oil but is the compound Spirit typified by the ointment formed by compounding a hin of olive oil with four spices—myrrh and cinnamon (signifying Christ's death with its effectiveness) and calamus and cassia (signifying Christ's resurrection with its power). As the compounded, all-inclusive, life-giving Spirit, He is now an ointment compounded with the four factors of God, man, Christ's death, and Christ's resurrection.

Christ's Two Becomings

The compounding of the Spirit took place when Christ as the last Adam became the life-giving Spirit. This becoming was not a simple matter. As we pointed out in the previous message, Christ has passed through two becomings. The first becoming was His incarnation: "The Word became flesh" (John 1:14). This becoming was rather simple, for it involved the entering of divinity into humanity and the mingling of divinity with humanity, but it did not include either death or resurrection. Christ's second becoming was His becoming in resurrection: "The last Adam became a life-giving Spirit" (1 Cor. 15:45b). This becoming was quite complicated because it included divinity, humanity, Christ's death, and Christ's resurrection.

*The Complications Involved in Christ's Death

Christ's death was itself very complicated. His death was an all-inclusive death. In His all-inclusive death He crucified the flesh of sin (Gal. 5:24; Rom. 8:3b); condemned sin and took away sin and sins by shedding His blood (Rom. 8:3b; John 1:29; Heb. 9:26b, 28a; John 19:34b); destroyed the devil, who has the might of death (Heb. 2:14; John 12:31b); judged the world and cast out its ruler (John 12:31; Gal. 6:14b); crucified

INCARNATION, INCLUSION, INTENSIFICATION   17

the old man (Rom. 6:6; Gal. 2:20a; 6:14b); terminated the old creation by the crucifixion of the old man (Rom. 6:6); abolished the law of the commandments in ordinances (Eph. 2:15a); and released the divine life (John 12:24; 19:34b). On the one hand, Christ's death dealt with all the negative things; on the other hand, His death released the divine life. The more we consider this, the more we will realize the complications involved in the Lord's all-inclusive death.

*The Complications Involved in Christ's Resurrection

Christ's resurrection was also very complicated. His resurrection produced the firstborn Son of God by uplifting the humanity of Christ into His divinity and by having Christ born of God (Acts 13:33; Psa. 2:7), that is, by designating the seed of David (Christ's human nature) by the Spirit of holiness (the divinity of Christ) in the power of resurrection to be the firstborn Son of God (Rom. 1:3-4). In Christ's resurrection all of God's chosen people were regenerated to be the many sons of God and the many brothers of the firstborn Son of God (1 Pet. 1:3; Heb. 2:10; Rom. 8:29). In Christ's resurrection the Spirit of God was consummated to be the life-giving Spirit (1 Cor. 15:45b): the Spirit of Christ—the pneumatic Christ, the pneumatized Christ (Rom. 8:9); the ultimate consummation of the processed and consummated Triune God, who is embodied in the pneumatized Christ as the life-giving Spirit; and the reality of resurrection, which is Christ Himself and the processed and consummated Triune God (John 11:25; 1 John 5:6). From this we can see that Christ's resurrection is full of complications.

Because so many complications are involved in Christ's second becoming, His becoming the all-inclusive life-giving Spirit in resurrection, we may use the word *inclusion* in speaking of this second stage of Christ. The issue of this becoming was not something simple but something compounded, that is, not just oil signifying the Spirit of God but the ointment signifying the life-giving Spirit, the Spirit who gives life. This Spirit is the pneumatic Christ, the Christ in the second stage—the stage of inclusion.

Whereas it is common for Christians to teach concerning

incarnation, very few, if any, teach concerning inclusion. The incarnation issued in the Christ who was in the flesh, but the inclusion has issued in a Christ who has become the compound, all-inclusive, life-giving Spirit. We see this compound Spirit in the book of Acts and in the twenty-one Epistles from Romans to Jude.

Christ in the First Stage Producing a Group of Redeemed Persons and Christ in the Second Stage Producing the Church

In the first stage, the stage of Christ in the flesh, Christ produced a group of redeemed persons, such as Peter and all the other disciples. Although a redeemed people had been produced, the church had not yet been produced. The church was produced by Christ in the second stage. In this stage Christ is the pneumatic Christ, the compound, life-giving Spirit who produced the church on the day of Pentecost. The redeemed saints, who were produced by Christ in the flesh, became the church produced by Christ as the life-giving Spirit.

The Third Stage—Intensification—the Stage of Christ as the Sevenfold Intensified Spirit

To Deal with the Degradation of the Church

Shortly after the church was produced, it began to become degraded. This is clearly seen in Acts. In chapter five Ananias and Sapphira lied to the Holy Spirit; in chapter six there was a murmuring of the Hellenists against the Hebrews regarding the daily dispensing; and in chapter fifteen there was trouble concerning circumcision. The separation of Barnabas from Paul (15:35-39) should also be regarded as a part of the degradation. Eventually the church degraded to such an extent that the Lord could no longer tolerate it, and He reacted by intensifying Himself sevenfold to become the sevenfold intensified Spirit (Rev. 1:4; 5:6). He became intensified sevenfold to deal with the degradation of the church.

To Produce the Body of Christ to Consummate the New Jerusalem

In his Epistles Paul spoke about the Body (Rom. 12:5; 1 Cor. 12:12, 27; Eph. 1:23; 4:4, 16; Col. 2:19), but I do not believe that Paul saw the actual building up of the Body. Paul could see the church expressed in various localities, but he could not see, in actuality, the church as the Body in a perfect and complete way. In order for the Body to be produced in a full and complete way, there is the need of the third stage of Christ, the stage of intensification in which Christ becomes the sevenfold intensified Spirit.

After Paul died, the Lord waited more than twenty years until John wrote the book of Revelation. Revelation is an Epistle, but it is very different in character from all the other Epistles in the New Testament. In this book Christ, who became the compound, all-inclusive, life-giving Spirit, has become the sevenfold intensified Spirit. In Revelation 1:4 the third of the Divine Trinity, the Spirit, becomes the seven Spirits and is ranked as the second of the Divine Trinity.

We have pointed out that in His second stage, the stage of His being the compound, all-inclusive, life-giving Spirit, Christ has produced the churches, but not much of the Body was produced and built up in an actual and practical way. For this reason, Christ has become the sevenfold intensified Spirit to overcome the degradation of the church that the overcomers may be produced to bring forth the Body.

The issue of Christ in the flesh was a group of redeemed persons, and the issue of Christ as the compound, all-inclusive, life-giving Spirit was the churches. For the Body to be produced there is the need for the compound, all-inclusive, life-giving Spirit to be intensified sevenfold. This sevenfold intensification deals with the sevenfold situation of the seven churches in Revelation 2 and 3.

The Brethren and those who followed their teaching saw something concerning the prophetic significance of the seven churches in Revelation 2 and 3. From their study of these chapters, they discovered that the church is in seven conditions, in seven stages, and in seven periods of time. However, they did not see the matter of overcoming. Jessie Penn-Lewis saw this matter and published a paper called *The Overcomer*. Although Mrs. Penn-Lewis wrote something concerning the seven churches producing the overcomers, the light she received was not full, and thus she did not see that the overcomers are for the building up of the Body to consummate the New Jerusalem. The stage of incarnation produced a group of redeemed people, and the stage of inclusion produced the church. The stage of intensification will build up the Body to consummate the New Jerusalem.

DOING A WORK OF THREE SECTIONS

I am burdened that all the co-workers in the Lord's recovery would realize that we need to do a work of three sections. We should not only be able to do the work of the first section, the section of incarnation, to produce redeemed people, but we should also be able to do a work that can serve the purpose of the second section, the section of inclusion, to produce churches. Furthermore, we should be able to do a work to build up the Body of Christ consummating the New Jerusalem. This is the work of the stage of intensification.

The first stage—incarnation—is in the physical realm for the accomplishment of judicial redemption, which is a physical matter. The second stage—inclusion—is divine and mystical. In the third stage—intensification—there will be a maturing and a ripening in the divine and mystical realm, and the Body will be built up to consummate the New Jerusalem.

In releasing this message, I am concerned that the co-workers are not carrying out a threefold work: the work in the stage of incarnation, the work in the stage of inclusion, and the work in the stage of intensification. If we are carrying out this threefold work, we will work not only to produce redeemed ones and work to establish churches but will also work to build up the Body consummating the New Jerusalem.

I would ask the co-workers to consider what kind of work they have done in the past and ask themselves if they have been doing a work of three sections. Regarding my own work I can say that the work which I did in mainland China was mainly to produce redeemed people. Only a small part of my work there was for the producing of churches. This indicates that my work in China was mainly a work in the first stage. However, when I came to Taiwan, I began to do a work in the stage of inclusion, and many churches were raised up. Now I am burdened to carry out a work in the stage of intensification. Therefore, I pray to the Lord, saying, "Lord, I am endeavoring to do my best to be an overcomer for the building up of Your Body to consummate the New Jerusalem."

I hope that all the co-workers will see the three stages, the three sections, of Christ: incarnation—the stage of Christ in the flesh; inclusion—the stage of Christ as the life-giving Spirit; and intensification—the stage of Christ as the sevenfold intensified life-giving Spirit. These three stages are the three sections of Christ's history. This means that Christ's history is divided into the section of His incarnation, the section of His inclusion, and the section of His intensification. Therefore we emphasize these three words—*incarnation, inclusion,* and *intensification*—and stress the facts that incarnation produces redeemed people, that inclusion produces the churches, and that intensification produces the overcomers to build up the Body, which consummates in the New Jerusalem as the unique goal of God's economy. This is the revelation in the New Testament.

What kind of work should we be doing today? We should be doing a work of all three sections. I am concerned that many of the co-workers are still working only in the first section, the section of incarnation. If this is your situation, you need to improve and to advance. What you have learned and what you have done in the past are not adequate. Of course, you should not discard the things of the first stage, for those things are the foundation. Now you need to begin building on this foundation and eventually have the completion of the building. The foundation is the work in the stage of incarnation; the building up is the work in the stage of inclusion; and the completion of the building is the work in the stage of intensification.

ADVANCING FROM INCLUSION TO INTENSIFICATION

My use of the word *inclusion* is based on our use of the word *inclusive*. For the last Adam to become the life-giving Spirit was for Christ to become the all-inclusive Spirit. His becoming all-inclusive was a matter not just of incarnation but of inclusion. As we have pointed out, inclusion involves many complications. In the stage of inclusion, many things are included in the pneumatic Christ, in the Christ who is the life-giving Spirit. Now we need to see that the all-inclusive, life-giving Spirit has been intensified sevenfold.

I would urge you to consider this matter of intensification and to pray desperately, saying, "Lord, I must advance. I need Your grace to bring me onward. I do not want to remain in the work of incarnation nor even in the work of inclusion. I want to advance from inclusion to intensification. Lord, You have been intensified sevenfold, and I pray that I also will be intensified sevenfold to overcome the degradation of the church that the Body may be built up to consummate the New Jerusalem."

CHAPTER THREE

AN EXTRACT OF THE BASIC DIVINE REVELATION IN THE HOLY SCRIPTURES

OUTLINE

I. To know the processed and consummated Triune God—Matt. 28:19:
   A. Incarnated to be the flesh—the first God-man to express God in humanity—John 1:14.
   B. Anointed to be the Christ, the anointed One of God, to accomplish God's plan in His eternal economy—Luke 4:18.
   C. Consummated to be the life-giving Spirit to apply what Christ has accomplished—1 Cor. 15:45b.
II. To know the all-inclusive Christ:
   A. As the mystery of God to be the reality of the Triune God—Col. 2:2.
   B. As the Word of God to define God—John 1:1.
   C. As the embodiment of God to express God—Col. 2:9.
   D. As the centrality and universality of God's eternal economy—Col. 1:13-19.
   E. As the God-allotted portion to be the enjoyment of His believers—Col. 1:12.
   F. As the life to His believers for them to live Him—Col. 3:4.
   G. As the Head of His Body for His expression—Col. 1:18.
III. To know the consummated Spirit:
   A. As the transfiguration of Christ in resurrection—1 Cor. 15:45b.

- B. As the compound Spirit, compounded with Christ's divinity, humanity, death with its effectiveness, and resurrection with its power as the elements to be the holy anointing ointment—Exo. 30:23-25.
- C. As the Spirit of life—Rom. 8:2.
- D. As the Spirit of God—Rom. 8:9.
- E. As the Spirit of Jesus—Acts 16:7.
- F. As the Spirit of Christ—Rom. 8:9.
- G. As the Spirit of Jesus Christ—Phil. 1:19.
- H. As the indwelling Spirit—Rom. 8:11.
- I. As the pneumatic Christ—Rom. 8:10.

IV. To know the church:
- A. As the universal house of God to be God's manifestation in humanity—1 Tim. 3:15-16.
- B. As the local churches to be the expression of the one church of God—Rev. 1:11; 1 Cor. 10:32.
- C. As the universal Body of Christ to be His fullness—Eph. 1:22-23.

V. To know the Body of Christ:
- A. The mystery of Christ—Eph. 3:4.
- B. The fullness of Him who fills all in all—Eph. 1:23.
- C. The organism of the Triune God, constituted with the Triune God and the believers—Eph. 4:4-6.
- D. The contents of the new man—Col. 3:10-11.
- E. To be built up by the perfected saints in all the local churches—Eph. 4:11-12.
- F. Not divided and not divisible—1 Cor. 1:10-13.
- G. To consummate the New Jerusalem.

VI. To know the ultimate consummation—the New Jerusalem—Rev. 21:
- A. A mystical constitution constituted with the processed and consummated Triune God with His chosen, redeemed, regenerated, transformed, and glorified people.
- B. As the bride—the wife—of the Lamb—vv. 2, 9.
- C. As the tabernacle to be the eternal dwelling place of God—v. 3.
- D. As the temple to be the eternal dwelling place of the glorified saints—v. 22.

THE BASIC DIVINE REVELATION 25

E. As the eternal expansion and expression of the processed and consummated Triune God in the regenerated, transformed, and glorified humanity.

VII. To know the self:
   A. As the old man, the natural man:
      1. Crucified with Christ on the cross—Gal. 2:20.
      2. Buried with Christ in baptism—Rom. 6:4.
   B. To be denied, condemned, and rejected all the time—Matt. 16:24.

In this message I would like to present an extract of the basic divine revelation in the Holy Scriptures. The seven points of this extract may be regarded as an extract of our theology. If you study all these points, you will see that the theology in the Lord's recovery is much different from all the theologies in today's Christianity.

I. TO KNOW THE PROCESSED AND CONSUMMATED TRIUNE GOD

First, we need to know the processed and consummated Triune God (Matt. 28:19).

A. Incarnated to Be the Flesh

The Triune God was incarnated to be the flesh (John 1:14). Through incarnation He became the first God-man, the Lord Jesus, and as such He expressed God in His humanity.

B. Anointed to Be the Christ

God was incarnated to be a God-man, and this God-man was anointed to be the Christ, the anointed One of God, to accomplish God's plan in His eternal economy (Luke 4:18). Actually, it was God Himself who came to accomplish what He had planned in eternity according to His eternal economy.

C. Consummated to Be the Life-giving Spirit

The Triune God has been consummated to be the life-giving Spirit to apply what Christ has accomplished (1 Cor. 15:45b). God the Father planned; God the Son accomplished what God the Father planned; and God the Spirit applies what God the Son has accomplished according to God the Father's plan.

II. TO KNOW THE ALL-INCLUSIVE CHRIST

Next we need to know the all-inclusive Christ in many different aspects.

A. The Mystery of God

We need to know the all-inclusive Christ as the mystery of God to be the reality of the Triune God (Col. 2:2). Christ is both the mystery of God and the reality of God. Embodied in

Christ is all that God is and has. All that God intends to do is related to Christ. If we do not know this Christ, we do not know God. We may say that Christ is the key that opens up the way into God. When we have Christ, God is open to us. Through Him we know God and even are brought into God. In Colossians 2:2 Paul speaks of "the mystery of God, Christ." The fact that Christ is the mystery of God indicates that He is not simple. On the contrary, He is immeasurable and mysterious. To be sure, God is not simple. He is unlimited, infinite, eternal. How, then, could Christ, the mystery of God, be simple? As the mystery of God, Christ is the immeasurable, infinite, and eternal God.

B. The Word of God

God is mysterious, and He needs the Word to define Him. The all-inclusive Christ is the Word of God to define God (John 1:1). As the Word of God He speaks God, and He is thereby the definition, explanation, and expression of God. As the Word Christ is God defined, explained, and expressed. The Word, therefore, is actually God Himself, not God hidden, concealed, and mysterious but God defined, explained, and expressed.

C. The Embodiment of God

The all-inclusive Christ is the embodiment of God to express God. "In Him dwells all the fullness of the Godhead bodily" (Col. 2:9). Before Christ's incarnation, the fullness of the Godhead dwelt in Him as the eternal Word, but it did not dwell in Him bodily. From the time that Christ became incarnate, clothed with a human body, the fullness of the Godhead began to dwell in Him in a bodily way, and in His glorified body (Phil. 3:21) now and forever it dwells. The Christ who is the embodiment of God not only speaks God and defines God—He also expresses God. Because He is the solid embodiment of God, He presents God to us, expressing Him.

D. The Centrality and Universality

The Christ who is the mystery of God, the reality of God, the definition of God, and the expression of God is also the universality and centrality of God's eternal economy

(Col. 1:13-19). In God's economy Christ is the center and the circumference.

God's economy may be likened to a great wheel, having Christ as its every part. Christ is the hub, the center of this wheel. "All things cohere in Him" (v. 17). This means that just as the spokes of a wheel are held together by the hub at their center, so all things exist together by Christ as the hub, the holding center. In the wheel of God's economy, Christ is also the spokes, the support, and the rim, the circumference.

E. The God-allotted Portion

We need to know the all-inclusive Christ as the God-allotted portion to be the enjoyment of His believers. Colossians 1:12 speaks of Christ as "the allotted portion of the saints." This refers to the lot of the inheritance, as illustrated by the allotment of the good land of Canaan given to the children of Israel for their inheritance (Josh. 14:1). The New Testament believers' inheritance, their God-allotted portion, is the all-inclusive Christ.

F. The Life to His Believers

Christ is the life to His believers for them to live Him. Colossians 3:4 speaks of "Christ our life." The life which is God, the life that God is, is in Christ (John 1:4). The Lord Jesus Himself said that He is life (John 11:25) and that He came that we may have life (John 10:10). Therefore, he who has Christ has life (1 John 5:12), and Christ now dwells in the believers as their life. Not only is the all-inclusive Christ our portion that we may enjoy Him; He is also life that we may live Him.

G. The Head of His Body

We need to know Christ as the Head of His Body to express Him. Colossians 1:18 says, "He is the Head of the Body, the church." Christ needs an expression. On the one hand, He expresses God; on the other hand, He is expressed by the Body. The Head expresses God, and the Body expresses the Head. Because Christ is the Head of the Body, we need to hold the Head so that the Body may grow with the growth of God (2:19). For the Body to hold the Head means that the Body does not allow itself to be separated from the Head. If we truly hold Christ as the Head of the Body, we will not be separated from Him by anything.

III. TO KNOW THE CONSUMMATED SPIRIT

Next, we need to know the consummated Spirit.

A. The Transfiguration of Christ

The consummated Spirit is the transfiguration of Christ in resurrection (1 Cor. 15:45b). Christ is the embodiment of God, and the Spirit is the transfiguration of Christ. In resurrection Christ, the last Adam in the flesh, became the life-giving Spirit. Christ's resurrection was His transfiguration into the life-giving Spirit. He was the Christ in the flesh, but through resurrection He was transfigured into the Christ who is the life-giving Spirit.

B. The Compound Spirit

The compound Spirit is the Spirit compounded with Christ's divinity, humanity, death with its effectiveness, and resurrection with its power typified by the elements of the holy anointing ointment in Exodus 30:23-25. According to the type in Exodus 30, the anointing ointment was a compound of one main item—a hin of olive oil—compounded with four spices: myrrh, cinnamon, calamus, and cassia. In typology, oil signifies the Spirit of God; flowing myrrh, Christ's death; cinnamon, the sweetness and effectiveness of Christ's death; calamus, Christ's resurrection; and cassia, the power, especially the repelling power, of Christ's resurrection. The type of the anointing ointment has been fulfilled completely in the life-giving Spirit, containing Christ's divinity, humanity, the sweetness and effectiveness of His death, and the power and effectiveness of His resurrection. The life-giving Spirit, therefore, is the compound Spirit.

C. The Spirit of Life

The Spirit is not only the life-giving Spirit but also the Spirit of life (Rom. 8:2). The Spirit of life is the reality of life, for this Spirit contains the element of the divine life. Actually, the Spirit Himself is life. Therefore, with the Spirit of life we have the riches of the divine life.

The way to have life is the Spirit. Life belongs to the Spirit, and the Spirit is of life. The two are actually one. We cannot separate life from the Spirit, nor the Spirit from life. If we have the Spirit, we have life. If we do not have the Spirit, we do not have life. The way to experience the divine, eternal, uncreated life is the Spirit of life.

D. The Spirit of God

In Romans 8:9 Paul speaks of the Spirit of God dwelling in us, and in verse 14, of the sons of God being led by the Spirit of God. We should not understand the title *the Spirit of God* to mean that the Spirit is something from God. In the New Testament phrases such as *the love of God* and *the life of God* mean that love and life are God Himself. In the same principle, the term *the Spirit of God* means that the Spirit is God. Hence, for us to be indwelt and led by the Spirit of God means that we are indwelt and led by God Himself.

E. The Spirit of Jesus

The Spirit of Jesus (Acts 16:7) is a particular expression concerning the Spirit of God and refers to the Spirit of the incarnated Savior who, as Jesus in His humanity, passed through human living and death on the cross. This indicates that the Spirit of Jesus contains not only the divine element but also the human element and the elements of Jesus' human living and His suffering of death.

F. The Spirit of Christ

In Romans 8:9 Paul speaks of the Spirit of Christ. The Spirit of Christ is related to the Lord's death and resurrection. The Spirit of Christ is the Spirit of the One who passed through death and entered into resurrection. The Spirit of Christ is the totality, the aggregate, of the all-inclusive Christ with His all-inclusive death and resurrection.

G. The Spirit of Jesus Christ

The Spirit of Jesus Christ (Phil. 1:19) is "the Spirit" mentioned in John 7:39. This is not merely the Spirit of God before the Lord's incarnation but the Spirit of God, the Holy Spirit with divinity, after the Lord's resurrection, compounded with the Lord's humanity, human living under the cross, crucifixion, and resurrection.

Because the Spirit of Jesus has particular reference to the Lord's suffering, and the Spirit of Christ to His resurrection, the Spirit of Jesus Christ is related to both His suffering and His resurrection. The Spirit of Jesus Christ is the Spirit of the Jesus who lived a life of suffering on earth and of the Christ who is now in resurrection. The reality of such a Jesus and such a Christ is the Spirit of Jesus Christ.

H. The Indwelling Spirit

The consummated Spirit is also the indwelling Spirit. In Romans 8:9 and 11 Paul speaks of the Spirit indwelling the believers. Verse 9 speaks of the Spirit of God dwelling in us, and verse 11 goes on to say, "If the Spirit of the One who raised Jesus from the dead dwells in you, He who raised Christ Jesus from the dead will also give life to your mortal bodies through His Spirit who indwells you." As the Spirit indwells us, He is active to impart life to us. The indwelling Spirit imparts the divine life into our tripartite being (vv. 10, 6, 11). The purpose of the Spirit's indwelling is to impart, to dispense, life, which is actually God Himself, into the three parts of our being.

I. The Pneumatic Christ

Finally, we need to know the consummated Spirit as the pneumatic Christ (Rom. 8:10). The pneumatic Christ is the Christ who is the life-giving Spirit. The Christ who was in the flesh went through death and resurrection to become the life-giving Spirit, the pneumatic Christ. Not only has Christ become the Spirit, the pneumatic Christ, but when He comes to us, He comes as the pneumatic Christ. Thus, when we receive Christ today, we receive Him as the pneumatic Christ, as the life-giving Spirit.

IV. TO KNOW THE CHURCH

The next matter that we need to know is the church.

A. The House of God

The church is the universal house of God to be God's manifestation in humanity (1 Tim. 3:15-16). In 1 Timothy 3:15 Paul speaks of "the house of God, which is the church of the living God." As God's dwelling place, the church is both God's house and His household, His family. In the Old Testament the temple and God's people were two separate things, but in the fulfillment in the New Testament the dwelling place of God and the family of God are one. Verses 15 and 16 indicate that the church as the house of God is also the manifestation of God in the flesh—the mystery of godliness. God is manifested in the church, the Body of Christ and the house of the living God, as the enlarged, corporate expression in the flesh, that is, in humanity.

B. The Local Churches

It is important that we know the church as the local churches to be the expression of the one church of God (Rev. 1:11; 1 Cor. 10:32). The church has both a universal aspect and a local aspect. In the local aspect the church is expressed in many localities as many local churches. The one universal church expressed in many places on earth becomes the many local churches. The expression of the church in a locality is the local church in that particular locality.

The universal church as the Body of Christ is expressed through the local churches. The local churches, as the expressions of the one Body of Christ, are locally one. Without the local churches there would be no practicality and actuality of the universal church. The universal church is realized in the local churches.

C. The Body of Christ

In its universal aspect the church is the universal Body

THE BASIC DIVINE REVELATION 33

of Christ to be His fullness. In Ephesians 1:22-23 Paul speaks of "the church, which is His Body, the fullness of the One who fills all in all." This is the church in its universal aspect, for Christ has only one Body, which is unique in the universe. Christ's universal Body is His fullness, His expression.

V. TO KNOW THE BODY OF CHRIST

In addition to knowing the church, we need to know the Body of Christ.

A. The Mystery of Christ

The Body of Christ is the mystery of Christ (Eph. 3:4). The mystery of God in Colossians 2:2 is Christ; the mystery of Christ in Ephesians 3:4 is the church. God is a mystery, and Christ, as the embodiment of God to express Him, is the mystery of God. Christ also is a mystery, and the church, as the Body of Christ, is the mystery of Christ. This mystery is God's economy, which is to dispense Christ, as the embodiment of God, into God's chosen people in order to produce a Body to be the increase of God's embodiment in Christ so that God may have a corporate expression.

B. The Fullness of the One Who Fills All in All

The Body of Christ is the fullness of Him who fills all in all (Eph. 1:23). It is the universal expression of the all-inclusive and all-extensive Christ. The Body as Christ's fullness is the fullness of Him who fills all in all. Christ, who is the infinite God without limitation, is so great that He fills all things in all things. Such a great Christ needs the Body to be His fullness for His complete expression.

C. The Organism of the Triune God

The Body of Christ is the organism of the Triune God, constituted with the Triune God and the believers (Eph. 4:4-6). The divine life is a substance, the Triune God, and the organism of the Triune God is the visible expression of this substance. Therefore, as the organism of the Triune God, the Body of Christ is altogether organic and is absolutely of life. An illustration of this organism is found in John 15—the vine with its branches. The vine is developed and enlarged through its branches. This is a picture of the Body of Christ as the organism of the Triune God, an organism that grows with the riches of the Triune God and expresses the divine life.

The organism of the Triune God, the Body of Christ, is an issue of the Divine Trinity; it is an issue of the Father as the source, the Son as the course, and the Spirit as the flow. Furthermore, the Body is constituted with the Triune God and the believers. In this constitution the Father is the source, the Son is the element, the Spirit is the essence, and the believers, God's redeemed and regenerated people, are the outward framework. The Father as the source, the Son as the element, and the Spirit as the essence are all in the outward framework.

D. The Contents of the New Man

The Body of Christ is the contents of the new man. Colossians 3:10 and 11 tell us that in the new man "Christ is all and in all." In the new man there is room only for Christ. He is all the members of the new man and in all the members. He is everything in the new man. Actually, He is the new man, His Body (1 Cor. 12:12). In the new man He is the centrality and universality. He is the constituent of the new man, and He is all in all in the new man.

E. To Be Built Up

The Body of Christ needs to be built up by the perfected saints in all the local churches (Eph. 4:11-12). Ephesians 4:11 speaks of the gifted persons—apostles, prophets, evangelists, and shepherds and teachers. These gifted persons have only one ministry, that is, to minister Christ for the building up of the Body of Christ, the church. Whatever the gifted persons do must be for the building up of the Body of Christ. However, this building up is not accomplished directly by the gifted ones but by the saints who have been perfected by them.

F. Not Divided

The Body of Christ is not divided and is not divisible. This is indicated clearly by Paul's word in 1 Corinthians 1:10-13.

THE BASIC DIVINE REVELATION   35

G. To Consummate the New Jerusalem

The building up of the Body of Christ consummates the New Jerusalem. Today we are building up the Body of Christ for the building up of the New Jerusalem. We are building up something in this age—the Body of Christ—that is for something in the next age—the New Jerusalem.

VI. TO KNOW THE ULTIMATE CONSUMMATION— THE NEW JERUSALEM

We need to advance from knowing the Body of Christ to knowing the ultimate consummation—the New Jerusalem (Rev. 21).

A. A Mystical Constitution

The New Jerusalem is a mystical constitution constituted with the processed and consummated Triune God with His chosen, redeemed, regenerated, sanctified, renewed, transformed, built-up, conformed, and glorified people.

B. The Bride

As such a mystical and organic constitution, the New Jerusalem is the bride—the wife—of the Lamb (Rev. 21:2, 9). This means that the New Jerusalem will be the counterpart of Christ, the embodiment of the processed and consummated Triune God. On the one-thousand-year wedding day (19:7-9) the New Jerusalem will be only the bride of the Lamb, but in eternity the New Jerusalem will be the Lamb's wife.

C. The Tabernacle

The New Jerusalem is also the tabernacle to be the eternal dwelling place of God. Revelation 21:3 says clearly that the New Jerusalem, the holy city, is the tabernacle of God. This indicates that the New Jerusalem is God's dwelling place. God's dwelling place is for His rest in expression. In the New Jerusalem God will have the utmost rest in expression for eternity.

The tabernacle made by Moses was a type of the New Jerusalem as God's eternal tabernacle (Exo. 25:8-9; Lev. 26:11).

This type was first fulfilled in Christ as God's tabernacle among men (John 1:14). He Himself was God's tabernacle. Eventually, the type of the tabernacle will be fulfilled in the fullest way in the New Jerusalem, which will be the enlargement of Christ as God's dwelling place.

D. The Temple

The New Jerusalem is the temple to be the eternal dwelling place of the glorified saints. Revelation 21:22b says, "The Lord God the Almighty and the Lamb are its temple." Since God and the Lamb are the temple, They cannot dwell in it, and it cannot be Their dwelling place. Rather, it is the dwelling place of the glorified saints, who serve the Triune God by dwelling in Him.

On the one hand, the New Jerusalem, which is composed of all the glorified saints, as the dwelling place of God, is the tabernacle. On the other hand, the New Jerusalem, which is constituted with the processed and consummated Triune God, as the dwelling place of the glorified saints, is the temple. Therefore, the New Jerusalem, being both the tabernacle and the temple, is the mutual dwelling place of the Triune God and the glorified saints.

E. The Eternal Expansion and Expression

The New Jerusalem is also the eternal expansion and expression of the processed and consummated Triune God in the regenerated, transformed, and glorified humanity. It is the spreading of the Triune God through His glorified saints as His increase for His eternal purpose. This spreading is illustrated by the vine with its branches in John 15. The branching out of the vine is the spreading of the vine. This is an illustration of the New Jerusalem as the expansion, the spreading, of the Triune God through His glorified saints.

VII. TO KNOW THE SELF

In addition to knowing the six foregoing matters, we need to know the self.

A. The Old Man, the Natural Man

In Romans 6:6 the *old man* refers to the natural life in our soul. The old man is our very being, which was created by God but became fallen through sin. It is the same as the "I" in Galatians 2:20. Our old man was crucified with Christ on the cross (Rom. 6:6; Gal. 2:20) and buried with Christ in baptism (Rom. 6:4). It is not the soul itself but the life of the soul which has been counted by God as hopeless and has been put on the cross and crucified with Christ.

B. Denying the Self

The self needs to be denied, condemned, and rejected all the time. In Matthew 16:24 the Lord Jesus said, "If anyone wants to come after Me, let him deny himself and take up his cross and follow Me." We, the believers in Christ, were crucified with Him, and now we need to bear the cross. For us to bear the cross means that we remain under the killing of the death of Christ for the terminating of our self, our natural life, and our old man. In so doing we deny our self that we may follow the Lord.

In this message we have covered, as an extract of the basic revelation in the Holy Scriptures, seven main matters in our theology: the Triune God, the all-inclusive Christ, the consummated Spirit, the church, the Body, the ultimate consummation (the New Jerusalem), and the self. We need to spend much time to study all these matters.

CHAPTER FOUR

THE GOD-MEN'S DIVINE RIGHT TO PARTICIPATE IN GOD'S DIVINITY

Scripture Reading: John 3:15; Col. 3:4; Eph. 1:4; 2 Pet. 1:4; Eph. 4:23; Phil. 2:5; 2 Cor. 3:18b; Eph. 3:8; 2 Cor. 3:18a; Rom. 8:29-30; Heb. 2:10; Eph. 1:5; Rom. 8:23, 19; 1 John 3:2; John 1:12; Rom. 8:14, 16

OUTLINE

I. To participate in God's life—John 3:15; Col. 3:4.
II. To participate in God's nature—Eph. 1:4; 2 Pet. 1:4.
III. To participate in God's mind—Eph. 4:23; Phil. 2:5.
IV. To participate in God's being—2 Cor. 3:18b; Eph. 3:8.
V. To participate in God's image—2 Cor. 3:18a; Rom. 8:29.
VI. To participate in God's glory—Rom. 8:30; Heb. 2:10.
VII. To participate in God's sonship—Eph. 1:5; Rom. 8:23.
VIII. To participate in God's manifestation—Rom. 8:19.
IX. To bear God's likeness—1 John 3:2.
X. To be Godkind—God's species—John 1:12; Rom. 8:14, 16.

In these days I am burdened to release the high-level truths in the Word, and I welcome every opportunity to do this. One of these high truths is the matter of participating in God's divinity. In this message I would like to give a brief word concerning the God-men's right to participate in God's divinity.

Number 473 in *Hymns* starts on a very basic level by encouraging us to be persons who are absolutely for God. This is good, but it is elementary. However, this hymn advances to a much higher level with a line in the third stanza which says, "He and you are one." How marvelous that we, fallen human beings, can be one with the Lord! Such a thought is surely very high. Now we need to see something even higher— that as God-men we have the divine right to participate in God's divinity.

The phrase *participate in* means not only to partake of but to partake of for enjoyment. It indicates that we possess something and that we enjoy what we possess. We, the God-men, have the divine right to participate not in heaven but in God's divinity. We all need to realize that we can participate in God's divinity, that is, participate in God.

We human beings were created by God for this purpose. Man was created in God's image and after His likeness (Gen. 1:26). We were created not in man's image and after man's likeness but in God's image and after God's likeness. Thus, human beings have the image and likeness of God. However, at the time of creation, man did not have God's life. But now as God-men, those who have been born of God to be children of God, we have the right to participate in what God is and even to become God in life, in nature, and in expression but not in the Godhead.

I. TO PARTICIPATE IN GOD'S LIFE

First, as the God-men we have the divine right to participate in God's life. John 3:15 tells us that everyone who believes in the Lord Jesus will have eternal life. Eternal life is the divine life, the life of God. We are human beings, but we can have God's life. We were created in God's image and God's likeness but without God's life. Through regeneration we have been graced by God with His divine life. Through regeneration He has put, has dispensed, His life into our being.

Colossians 3:4 speaks of "Christ our life." Since Christ is the embodiment of God, for Christ to be our life means that God is our life.

II. TO PARTICIPATE IN GOD'S NATURE

As God-men we also have the divine right to participate in God's nature. Ephesians 1:4 says, "He chose us in Him before the foundation of the world to be holy." Here we see that God chose us in Christ with a particular purpose—to make us holy. *Holy* means not only sanctified, separated unto God, but also different, distinct, from everything common. God is holy, but we are common. Only God is different, distinct, from all things. Hence, He is holy; holiness is His nature. God intends to make us holy even as He is holy (1 Pet. 1:15-16). To be holy is to participate in God's holy nature. Having chosen us to be holy, God makes us holy by imparting Himself, the Holy One, into our being, so that our whole being may be saturated and permeated with His holy nature. For us, God's chosen ones, to be holy is to partake of God's divine nature (2 Pet. 1:4). Thus, we may participate not only in God's life but also in God's nature.

III. TO PARTICIPATE IN GOD'S MIND

Because we have become God-men through regeneration, we also have the right to participate in God's mind. This means that we, who are human, can have a divine mind. Philippians 2:5 says, "Let this mind be in you, which was also in Christ Jesus." We need to let Christ's mind be our mind. In this way we may have Christ's mind.

Ephesians 4:23 says, "Be renewed in the spirit of your mind." The spirit here is the regenerated spirit of the believers, which is mingled with the indwelling Spirit of God. Such a mingled spirit spreads into our mind, thus becoming the spirit of our mind. The more the mingled spirit penetrates our mind, saturates our mind, and possesses our mind, the more our mind becomes like God's mind. This is to make His mind our mind, and this is to participate in God's mind.

IV. TO PARTICIPATE IN GOD'S BEING

Next, the God-men have the divine right to participate in God's being. Our basis for saying this is Paul's word in 2 Corinthians 3:18 about our being transformed into the Lord's image "even as from the Lord Spirit." This indicates that the work of transformation is done not by something of the Lord Spirit but by the Lord Spirit Himself. Hence, we are being transformed with God's very being.

In Ephesians 3:8 Paul speaks of the unsearchable riches of Christ, indicating that these riches have been dispensed into us. The unsearchable riches of Christ are the riches of Christ's being, the riches of what Christ is. For the unsearchable riches of Christ to be dispensed into us means that we participate not only in God's life, nature, and mind but also in His being.

V. TO PARTICIPATE IN GOD'S IMAGE

As God-men we also have the divine right to participate in God's image. Second Corinthians 3:18 says that we are being "transformed into the same image." This is the image of the resurrected and glorified Christ. In God's creation man was made in God's image in an outward way, but the image into which we are being transformed is something inward. To be transformed into the same image is to be conformed to the resurrected and glorified Christ as the firstborn Son of God, to be made the same as He is (Rom. 8:29).

Transformation is a kind of metabolism. The metabolism involved in transformation is comparable to that which takes place in our physical body after we eat, digest, and assimilate food. Transformation is the metabolic function of the divine life in the believers. We Christians, who are God-men, all have the Lord Spirit within us, and the Lord Spirit is in the process of carrying out a metabolic change in our being, transforming us into the image of Christ. To be metabolically transformed into the image of the resurrected and glorified Christ is to participate in God's image.

VI. TO PARTICIPATE IN GOD'S GLORY

Eventually, we will be brought into God's glory to participate in His glory. Hebrews 2:10 says that God is leading many sons into glory. Paul refers to this in Romans 8:30: "Those whom He predestinated, these He also called; and those whom He called, these He also justified; and those whom He justified, these He also glorified." Glorification is the step in God's complete salvation in which God will completely saturate our body with the glory of His life and nature. In this way He will transfigure our body, conforming it to the resurrected, glorious body of His Son (Phil. 3:21). This is the ultimate step in God's organic salvation, wherein God obtains a full expression, which will be manifested ultimately in the New Jerusalem.

VII. TO PARTICIPATE IN GOD'S SONSHIP

Another aspect of the God-men's divine right to participate in God's divinity is the right to participate in God's sonship (Eph. 1:5; Rom. 8:23). We can have God's life, God's nature, God's mind, God's being, God's image, and God's glory because we are God's sons. Just as a human son has the life, nature, mind, being, and image of his human father, so the sons of God have the life, nature, mind, being, and image of their divine Father. Furthermore, as a human son shares the glory or prestige of his human father, the sons of God share in the glory of their divine Father.

Ephesians 1:5 tells us God has predestinated us "unto sonship." The Greek word for *predestinating* in this verse may also be translated "marking out beforehand." Before the foundation of the world, that is, in eternity past, God predestinated us, marked us out, unto sonship. Before time began God intended and determined that we would participate in His sonship.

VIII. TO PARTICIPATE IN GOD'S MANIFESTATION

As God-men we will participate also in God's manifestation (Rom. 8:19). When Christ our life is manifested, we will be manifested with Him in glory (Col. 3:4.) Today God is hiding, but one day He will be manifested to the whole universe. Romans 8:19 indicates that when God is manifested, revealed, we, the sons of God, will participate in that revelation, in that manifestation. God will be manifested with His sons, who will be the same as He in life, in nature, in mind, in being, in image, and in glory.

IX. TO BEAR GOD'S LIKENESS

The God-men's divine right to participate in God's divinity includes the right to bear God's likeness. First John 3:2 says, "Beloved, now we are children of God, and it has not yet been manifested what we will be. We know that if He is manifested, we will be like Him because we will see Him even as He is." This clearly reveals that we will bear God's likeness. We will not only participate in God's life and nature but will also bear God's likeness. To bear God's likeness will be a great blessing and enjoyment.

X. TO BE GODKIND—GOD'S SPECIES

Finally, the God-men have the divine right to be Godkind—God's species (John 1:12; Rom. 8:14, 16). We have been regenerated to be Godkind. As God's sons we are God's kind, God's species.

John 1:12 says, "As many as received Him, to them He gave the authority to become children of God." We have received the Lord Jesus by believing into Him, and God has given us the authority, the right, to be God's children. "The Spirit Himself witnesses with our spirit that we are children of God" (Rom. 8:16). Such a witnessing testifies to us and assures us that we are children of God, who possess His life. We need to realize this and remember it. Wherever we may be we need to remember that we are God-men with the divine right to participate in God's divinity.

About the Author

Witness Lee was born in 1905 in northern China and raised in a Christian family. At age 19 he was fully captured for Christ and immediately consecrated himself to preach the gospel for the rest of his life. Early in his service, he met Watchman Nee, a renowned preacher, teacher, and writer. Witness Lee labored together with Watchman Nee under his direction. In 1934 Watchman Nee entrusted Witness Lee with the responsibility for his publication operation, called the Shanghai Gospel Bookroom.

Prior to the Communist takeover in 1949, Witness Lee was sent by Watchman Nee and his other co-workers to Taiwan to ensure that the things delivered to them by the Lord would not be lost. Watchman Nee instructed Witness Lee to continue the former's publishing operation abroad as the Taiwan Gospel Bookroom, which has been publicly recognized as the publisher of Watchman Nee's works outside China. Witness Lee's work in Taiwan manifested the Lord's abundant blessing. From a mere 350 believers, newly fled from the mainland, the churches in Taiwan grew to 20,000 in five years.

In 1962 Witness Lee felt led of the Lord to come to the United States, and he began to minister in Los Angeles. During his 35 years of service in the U.S., he ministered in weekly meetings and weekend conferences, delivering several thousand spoken messages. Much of his speaking has since been published as over 400 titles. Many of these have been translated into over fourteen languages. He gave his last public conference in February 1997 at the age of 91.

He leaves behind a prolific presentation of the truth in the Bible. His major work, *Life-study of the Bible,* comprises over 25,000 pages of commentary on every book of the Bible from the perspective of the believers' enjoyment and experience of God's divine life in Christ through the Holy Spirit. Witness Lee was the chief editor of a new translation of the New Testament into Chinese called the Recovery Version and directed the translation of the same into English. The Recovery Version also appears in a number of other languages. He provided an extensive body of footnotes, outlines, and spiritual cross references. A radio broadcast of his messages can be heard on Christian radio stations in the United States. In 1965 Witness Lee founded Living Stream Ministry, a non-profit corporation, located in Anaheim, California, which officially presents his and Watchman Nee's ministry.

Witness Lee's ministry emphasizes the experience of Christ as life and the practical oneness of the believers as the Body of Christ. Stressing the importance of attending to both these matters, he led the churches under his care to grow in Christian life and function. He was unbending in his conviction that God's goal is not narrow sectarianism but the Body of Christ. In time, believers began to meet simply as the church in their localities in response to this conviction. In recent years a number of new churches have been raised up in Russia and in many European countries.

Other Books Published By
Living Stream Ministry

Titles by Witness Lee:

Abraham—Called by God	978-0-7363-0359-0
The Experience of Life	978-0-87083-417-2
The Knowledge of Life	978-0-87083-419-6
The Tree of Life	978-0-87083-300-7
The Economy of God	978-0-87083-415-8
The Divine Economy	978-0-87083-268-0
God's New Testament Economy	978-0-87083-199-7
The World Situation and God's Move	978-0-87083-092-1
Christ vs. Religion	978-0-87083-010-5
The All-inclusive Christ	978-0-87083-020-4
Gospel Outlines	978-0-87083-039-6
Character	978-0-87083-322-9
The Secret of Experiencing Christ	978-0-87083-227-7
The Life and Way for the Practice of the Church Life	978-0-87083-785-2
The Basic Revelation in the Holy Scriptures	978-0-87083-105-8
The Crucial Revelation of Life in the Scriptures	978-0-87083-372-4
The Spirit with Our Spirit	978-0-87083-798-2
Christ as the Reality	978-0-87083-047-1
The Central Line of the Divine Revelation	978-0-87083-960-3
The Full Knowledge of the Word of God	978-0-87083-289-5
Watchman Nee—A Seer of the Divine Revelation...	978-0-87083-625-1

Titles by Watchman Nee:

How to Study the Bible	978-0-7363-0407-8
God's Overcomers	978-0-7363-0433-7
The New Covenant	978-0-7363-0088-9
The Spiritual Man • 3 volumes	978-0-7363-0269-2
Authority and Submission	978-0-7363-0185-5
The Overcoming Life	978-1-57593-817-2
The Glorious Church	978-0-87083-745-6
The Prayer Ministry of the Church	978-0-87083-860-6
The Breaking of the Outer Man and the Release...	978-1-57593-955-1
The Mystery of Christ	978-1-57593-954-4
The God of Abraham, Isaac, and Jacob	978-0-87083-932-0
The Song of Songs	978-0-87083-872-9
The Gospel of God • 2 volumes	978-1-57593-953-7
The Normal Christian Church Life	978-0-87083-027-3
The Character of the Lord's Worker	978-1-57593-322-1
The Normal Christian Faith	978-0-87083-748-7
Watchman Nee's Testimony	978-0-87083-051-8

Available at
Christian bookstores, or contact Living Stream Ministry
2431 W. La Palma Ave. • Anaheim, CA 92801
1-800-549-5164 • www.livingstream.com